FOOD

FOR

THE

SOUL

AND

HEART

ITUMELENG KEKANA

Food for the soul and heart

Itumeleng Kekana
Frank Sediko

2019

First Printing: 2019

Pretoria, South Africa

Contact: +27(62) 589 8179

ISBN: 978-0-359-69950-6

Email: tmlngkekana@gmail.com

Publisher : Itumeleng Kekana, Printer : Lulu

Acknowledgements

I would like to thank everyone who has supported me throughout the journey of this book. I would especially like to thank the following

Lawrence Kekana, Lolo Kekana, Lesibana Kekana, Joyce Thage, Gladys Thage, Amogelang Motlana, Boipelo Tlalang, Thoriso Taukubung, Tshegofatso Mabe, Junior Modimogale, Mpho Madlabane, Patrick Kekana, Chantel Khoza, Remoratile Mohlala, Olerato Taole, Gomotsegang Baloyi and Lethabo Lerumo.

I would also like to thank everyone in my life who I received some motivation and inspiration from, for that (motivation and inspiration) I would like to thank my Science Lecturer , Mr Nkuna , he told us (my class) that we are revolutionaries/ revolutionists but we shouldn't be enablers of violence, we should be thirsty for change, not only to change our country but the whole Africa, what he said that day has never left my heart. The second person is Letlhogonolo Phalane, he always pushes me to do more, to be more and third person is Frank Sediko, always makes sure I'm at the top of things that I'm always on my toes, that I'm exposed to a lot in order to grow.

To all my primary school teachers, thank you, not only was my talent moulded and nurtured at a very young age but I was also introduced to many things because my talent was nurtured well enough.

To all my high school teachers, one thing I've truly learnt is every journey has a story to tell and that everyone you come across in your journey has a purpose, some for good reasons and some for bad reasons, but I'd like to thank my grade 9-12 English teacher Ms N O'Connell, your love for novels and reading eventually rubbed on to me and I ended up writing my own book.

Everyone played a certain role in my life, from stimulating creativity to learning more about anything in life.

We didn't cross paths by chance or by mistake.

From the Apex of my heart I'd like to THANK ALL OF YOU.

Content

Planet E901

Chapter 2

Being one with nature

Chapter 3

Bonus poems

Introduction

At a personal level, food is closely connected to the central power of the human soul and memory. Religions say that when you eat certain food, God dwells within you, for instance , the ancient Greeks called it Omophagia [eating the god] which a dictionary explanation of this Omophagia is simply [the eating of raw food], Christians eat bread and drink wine knowing that sacramentally these foods will fill their souls with the divine, the Jewish Seder which is the longest meal you can ever have to sit through and also Islam's celebration after fasting for many days they celebrate by feasting.

Cooking is a good soul art, now how does poetry fit into all of this, well Poetry is one of the oldest artistic techniques of expressing emotions, where the poet opens to the reader which is basically like peeking into the poet's soul. Poetry is sentimental on many levels even though reality tells otherwise, some poets write to keep themselves 'sane'.

"I'm reliant on words, on poems because that's the only time I feel real"

This is FOOD FOR THE SOUL AND HEART.

This book is not like any other book on the shelves, this is one unique book with priceless content, this book connects souls, it shares emotions, it's your friend. I believe this book goes against the statement 'Actions speak louder than words'. I believe that this book is versatile and I advise you to read it with an open heart just as how this book is symbolizing me opening my heart to you, reason for this is that if you read this book without an open heart and an open mind the content will have no meaning, the content won't have any sentimental meaning and value and it will simply not be as " priceless"

I think to understand this book you should greatly be one with nature

You should acquire a great deal of all the elements that surround you because it's all about finding comfort in the most sensitive subjects to society. Don't forget we are society and there are certain 'norms' and taboo this is all about understanding yourself as an individual, the ultimate goal for this book was to connect and build relationships, the next goal was to show loyalty and appreciation to the things we seem to not show enough appreciation and loyalty to, basically to open minds , to show people to be self -aware.

1

This book was written for any gender, any age, for anyone but I want to stress a little issue ...

DON'T TAKE EVERYTHING WRITTEN TOO LITERAL,

MAY BE TOO THOUGHT PROVOKING,

BE OPEN MINDED AND OPEN HEARTED,

YOU CAN READ IT ANYWHERE, ANYTIME FOR ANY MOOD YOU WILL BE EXPERIENCING.

MESSAGE FROM AUTHOR

Well to begin with this is quite an honor mainly because I'm sharing my thoughts and views about my life. Some may say this book is a little bit too based on my opinions and how I perceive life based on my experience and age, some may say I am a little bit too naïve and too inexperienced but it's not about that , I honestly wrote this book because I've been told by many people that I am a talented writer, that I am very emotive so I wanted to see how far would I go to complete a book but it was also I think not by luck a way of expressing my emotions on certain topics, I honestly wanted to challenge myself. I came here with no expectations but to express myself, to try something new. There are topics which are becoming problematic not necessarily amongst the youth but amongst the human race: people are not expressing how they feel, literally they die with all their feelings bottled up.

The book's main purpose was to liberate those who are oppressed, those who are oppressed mentally, physically and spiritually. This book's main purpose was to be the voice to those who are not heard, honestly, me being a teenager or probably in my youth, I learned that it's hard to do certain things due to being oppressed by peer pressure, popular culture, lack of creativity because of certain behaviors linked to being creative. Writing this book was not only to motivate my fellow peers but to also motivate and inspire people of all ages to tap into their creative side and learn a few things from those who are exploring their creative side.

I'm not necessarily condoning teenagers over-populating the music industry talking about how they do drugs and get drunk at parties; this book is just one of the many ways to express one's creativity without partying and substance abuse.

Based on months and years of research I then came about officially writing this book. I have then come to an understanding that this book is a poem, one huge poem which has one goal, to express my thoughts about life in this modern day and to also share my life but in my own eyes. I seem to believe that there's more content this book contains than just poetry and after months of evaluating certain poems I then saw that it's all about being open minded and open hearted to truly see what I'm seeing. Well in this book I just try to let you into not only my mind but also to let you into my heart.

A little behind the scenes of the book

I started planning for this book on the 3rd of November 2016, but I started writing the majority of the content on the 3rd of November 2018. People (usual authors) have the tendencies of writing the whole book in a time frame of between 2 – 7 months, but the reason why I took so long was mainly because I had to maximize the emotions I express, what I mean is I wanted to make sure every poem in this book had a genuine uniqueness, originality and had synced with any of my emotions at that time, so therefore, this book has sentimental value beyond how I can explain, very meaningful to me and to the literature world out there.

During the writing of this book, I had huge support from a couple of people, my friends, family, everyone in my life, some may have not known that I was writing this book but they supported me. Whilst I was writing, I learnt quite a lot of things, relating to being an author. People think that getting the title of being an author is something simple, but on the contrary its quite difficult to achieve that title. To be honest it's not about the title , it's not about the fame of being an author, it's not about having a book to brag about, it's all about talent and finding yourself, whether it's something you would not mind doing as a career, but to be honest it's not even about it being a career.

After writing this book I honestly would not mind writing again, it's like having a tattoo; it starts with one but a person would not mind getting more. I enjoyed writing this book and I enjoyed reading it, I hope you also enjoy it as much as I did.

Enjoy.
Author
I. Kekana

The beginning of a new journey

Chapter 1

Poems in chapter 1 are thirty-three (33)

What's Life

what's life

life is too short

it's too short to take everything seriously

it's too short to not find happiness

life is an ongoing challenge

a challenge that strengthens your faith

a challenge that tests your loyalty

life is about caring

caring for everyone

caring for every living thing

always find a reason to be happy

always find a reason to smile

because happiness can heal all broken hearts

life is about being unique

life is about being yourself

that's just half of how I see life

but that's my perspective on life

what's life to you?

I.k

Insight

We all have different perspectives on life, how you see life may differ from how I see life but, life is more than what we can ever imagine thinking about it for a second there are about trillion living species on earth so there's honestly more to life the true meaning, is how you live your life. Well just to clear some air, due to cultural differences and religious differences, we tend to think we know the meaning of life, but honestly, I don't think it would be appropriate to argue about the meaning of life because of our cultural and religious differences, but all I can say is we will see life differently. What really matters is how you treat all living things around you, it's about how the little things matter to you, that shows how you live and how you see life. Most importantly it shows the meaning of life to you.

The youth

Things aren't the way they used to be

What's different is that back then the youth

Wasn't dying because of depression

But – because of oppression

But now - no

Slowly but surely one by one

They die in isolation

What's sad

About the youth is

The only way they live is by injecting substances

Sniffing their lives away

Drowning their lives, they survive by diluting

The minds with substances which –

Don't enhance their situation

But only makes matters worse

One can't rely on role models

Majority of the youth's role models are

Drug addicts, gangsters, rich drop-outs

Some feel forgotten

Some are broken but –

They are all broken with a common factor

An excessive amount of doubts, scars and

Mostly with tears too

Spending my years attending my peers' funerals

And the cause of death is common –

Depression-

The youth is dying the same way

Drug overdoses, hanging from ropes,

a bullet on the head

 funny how they are all complaining

about being forgotten but they don't

know they end up being an afterthought

when they have killed themselves

funny how they all cry

'we are too young –

Too young to be depressed

Too young to die'

that's not all, what's the world doing

nothing-

I've had a chance to learn that the mind

is powerful as it can build a person

but also break a person

what happened to the Nazi wasn't great depression

what's happening now with the youth that's

great depression

insight

honestly, the youth is at their most vulnerable and its quite scary, people are just dying. some slept and never woke up, some were involved in accidents, some killed, some overdosed and some killed themselves but honestly, I have never experienced such a constant death report about some child dying.

The temptation is also a huge factor as it's not hiding in the shadows as it used to, it's roaming freely on the streets, it's sold to kids to 'strengthen the economy'. to me, the youth is far from being weak the problem is that negativity and temptations have become stronger and nobody is changing the situation, no one is making the situation better.

What's even heart-breaking is knowing that yesterday your friend was happy and smiling with the words "friend I'm fine" and just to find out the following day your friend is no more.

Past + Present = future

Who are we?

We are the future of the past

We are the present

We are a gift

But we are afraid

That we will never escape

Escape from our past

We are afraid of what the future

Shall bring

We wait for the salt in the hourglass

To finish

Are we waiting for the end?

Are we waiting for success?

Are we waiting for love?

Are we waiting for hope and faith?

We are afraid that we won't succeed

We are afraid that we won't be loved

We have little faith in ourselves

We have little hope

We are the past

The present

And the future

Insight

It doesn't mean that we don't want to be successful, but I feel that we want to be too successful, it doesn't mean that we don't want to be loved but I feel that we don't want to be hurt , we want to be loved for every breath taken, it doesn't mean we don't have faith and hope, the problem is we have high expectations and little realization of reality.

We are afraid of taking a huge leap of faith towards success, we are afraid of taking a huge leap of faith towards love that's why some of us aren't successful. We are surrounded by opportunities and a lot of resources, but bravery is the department that lacks in achieving anything we want.

Think about it, investigate history how certain things were made, it's all based on stepping out of your comfort zone as an individual and having confidence in yourself, that's my definition of bravery.

My #1 fan

Dear fam, my number 1 fan

This is not just another poem

This is not just ink on a white pad

I hope everyone's good

I've been thinking of life

The wrong and the right

Even though sometimes I'm right

I can't seem to find the light

Dear fam, my number 1 fan

As I'm writing this letter

I'm trying to expand

I'm trying to be better than-

What I am

But on another note

This is not just another note

This is not just another poem

This is not just ink on a white pad

This is more of an oath

Dear fam, my number 1 fan

I'm writing this letter to say

Thank you for being there

Thank you for your support

Fam

I'm your number 1 fan

'Us'

It's a two-letter word-

It's a word which starts

With a 'U' and end with an 'S'

We were there for each other

It was Us against the world

But now

It's me against the world

You left me, and I turned into a poet

You left me, and I turned you into a poem

But you know me, I never run

I would never run from you

I would walk away slowly

So that you can stop me

But it kills me because

You don't care enough to stop me

Instead, you left, you ran

Faster than I could blink

You left me hanging

But don't worry I would never

Hang myself for what you did

And yet it was always you and I

It was us against the world

Us

The brightest star in the sky

You glow

Brighter than a full moon

On a summer's night

You are the brightest star in the universe

And you are standing right in front of me

Even though

We are not perfect

You are perfect

And beyond

Out of a trillion stars out there

There's only you

You are unique

You are beautiful

You are one in a trillion

You are there for me

When my days are dark

I sometimes hope if I am there for

You, when your days are dark

How I hope I'm your brightest star in the sky

Twinkle, twinkle

The brightest star in the sky

How I wonder if you are

One of the seven wonders

How I see a twinkle in your

Eyes with an innocent smile

How I know I'm your

brightest star in the sky

Insight

I wrote this poem for one of my close friends, she's more than just a friend, she's more of my number 1 fan, she's always there for me. I strongly believe that everyone must have a friend like her. She's more of the positivity I need in my life, she's that type of friend that one is highly protective of, she is that kind of friend who is more than just a friend she is more of a sister and I believe that some people do have such a friend, or they are such a friend, well to all the brightest stars in the sky's you guys bring beauty to the skies at night.

18:18:17

I'm out of site

Out of mind

Out of time to decide

Should I run, should I hide

For the rest of my life

No

You're out of time

Well it's time to

Face the music

They cannot do anything to you

Don't take that rage and bottle it

Instead

Crush that bottle with your

Bare hands and swallow it

When they come for you spit it

Right in their face

Just Do it

Don't fear them

Don't let them oppress you

They cannot do anything to you

It's about time you retaliate

They've done you wrong

Insight

I can't stress this enough DON'T TAKE EVERYTHING WRITTEN TOO LITERAL, this poem was written to express how I feel about bullying, how I feel for the bullied kids, I personally have not been bullied I don't know how it feels. The poem is honestly against any form of violence, it's a protest against bullying and it's there to motivate all bullied children or in fact anyone who feels bullied to retaliate, to not hide, to not shell themselves in but stand up for themselves and for others. NO BULLY SHALL conquer, we are meant to live with one another not against each other.

One hundred

One hundred years,

One century

One hundred years to fathom

One hundred years to self-discovery

Not necessarily one hundred years of loneliness

Because I have her

And even though the thought

Of her could fade and wither

I would still go crazy with tenderness

When I see her

For you

One hundred years is

One century and that's

Ten long decades that's

Ten long decades of loneliness

Ten long decades of self-destruction

Ten long decades of regrets

Because you thought you didn't

Deserve me

I was 'more of a blunt knife for you'

Those words still roam in my head

But this time it's more of

I'm too sharp for your blunt

Decisions, I'm too sharp for your blunt life

Insight

is it not ironic though? How we usually ignore the ones who adore us, how we usually adore the ones who ignore us, how we usually love the ones who hurt us, how we usually hurt the ones who love us, it's ironic how karma takes its course, How ironic...

Different breed

I contemplate

I meditate

I meditate for the mind

I meditate for the soul

I use meditation as a form

Of Medication

But for this generation

A need for elaboration?

This generation uses alcohol

Drugs and medication

To heal their minds and souls

Some sell their souls

For music and their goals

But I guess we are a

Different breed

September

I cry for you

I cry for you because

You come with change

You come with a new season

September, I've been waiting

For you

Because you look beautiful

With all the different flowers and colors

September you bring people

Together

You bring joy and smiles

And yet you are not highly

Celebrated

September, you are special

You are the brightest amongst them

Very vibrant

You ooze with positive energy

September You are the brightest day

After the dark, gloomy, cold day

September, I cry for you but

You put a smile on my face

What to do

What to do with what I know

I know everything but

I don't know what to do with

What I know

I know a lot but take a chance,

Put yourself in my shoes

I know a lot

I know me, I know you, I know there's us

I know without you and me, there's no us

I know originality

I know respect and loyalty

I know morality and spirituality

With gangsters, drug lords and depression

Lurking in every corner I know fatality

Intriguing,

I know wisdom, I know bad religion

I know the good and the bad

I know good people who are always sad

I know how the youth tries to end things

With an overdose of prescription, as if

It's all their decision to make

I know good karma

I know

I know how the universe works

I know everything

But is it all meant for me?

I know the education system doesn't

really liberate all

I know drop-outs

I know adrenaline junkies

I know druggies, I know 'honey'

But is it all meant for me?

Now tell me what to do with what I know

Or maybe it's not for you to know

But since you know

Do some self-introspection

Look into the mirror and ask yourself

What would you do?

Superman

I'm not highly celebrated

Even though I write to liberate them

I guess I should meditate on it then

I'm here to elevate them

Levitate them

Slightly dedicated, mostly passion

I'm passionate then

Ink on a white pad

I'm a superman version of Shakespeare

I'm a comet, I'm a sonnet

I'm a poet

All these poems on the table

In my head, slightly unstable

Are you able?

To understand, I've always been

That kid with emotions locked in the basement

I'm not highly celebrated

But I still write to liberate them

I'm a superman version of Shakespeare

Probably a black panther version of cummings or

Probably a Batman version of Rossetti or

Probably an ironman version of Campbell

I don't want to be celebrated though

Fame might spoil this talent

I'm a comet, I'm a sonnet

I'm a poet

I'm superman

I feel like funeral blues

My heart ice cold, a hard frost

But my poems warm my heart

Like the garden of love

But remember

I was never celebrated and

I don't want to be celebrated

I write to liberate them

I write to liberate you but

I'm only a poet

I'm not a superman

To you but

I'm more than that

I'm a sonnet, I'm a comet

I'm more of a

Superman

Symphony 5683

In my mind I'm fire

My heart is the lighter

My soul is the fluid

My poems spark an artistic poet

A poet with poemteristis

Or is it poetrytis

Like Beethoven composing a symphony

Emotions are flowing

A lot goes in

-to these poems

A lot goes in

-to these lines

Experience builds these rhymes

Talent works overtime

But no person is

Expecting a dime

Like Beethoven

I'm composing symphony no 5683

Insight

Symphony 5683, this is a first of many colorful poems to expect. Inspired by Beethoven, I wonder what Beethoven was thinking while composing his symphonies. I think the main theme in this poem was music is poetry but there are honestly a lot of themes to this poem.

Moonlight

I'm talking to the moon and stars

I'm talking to Venus about love

She said if it's not about love

You weren't be looking above

Flying high like a dove

She said you seem so close

Yet you are so far

Shining bright like a star

I'll ride with you until

The end

I swear it's not a lie

She's always saying it's him and me

I'm talking to the moon and stars

I'm talking to Venus about love

Sober as ever I'm not high

If it wasn't about love

You won't be looking above

Flying high like a dove

You seem so close

Yet so far

But you are shining bright like a star

Humans

We are socially connected

But we are lonely,

Emotionally and psychologically bothered

We claim to know the beginning

And predicted the end

Numerously

Do we know ourselves as clearly as?

We claim to

If so, then why

Are we filled with hatred?

Why are we so violent?

Why do we kill one another

There's no peace

Where's the white flag in the warzone

Why are we so violent?

We seem to be drifting apart

Just like our continents have

It seems that this world is ruled by

Depression and anxiety

We are alienated by society

But it seems that the loneliest people tend

To be gentle and kind

It seems that most damaged people tend

To be the wisest

It seems that the saddest people tend

To bring the warmest and brightest smiles

This is a tragedy

For the humankind

As death seems to be targeting the stress less

The happy and the young

It's not really preying on the weak

Not really survival of the fittest

Honestly, death is not the greatest tragedy

Human actions are the greatest tragedy

Humans with inhumane behaviors

An hour

Who's going to put back

The pieces to my broken heart

Strangers can become best friends just as easily

As best friend can be strangers

We live in a place where being honest

Won't get you a lot of friends

But I hope it will get you the right ones

It's funny

Funny how they think I'm doing this for

Fame and money

Funny how they don't see my true intentions

Funny how they think I'm 'pulling moves'

As all of this is a game of monopoly

On the next move as

They claim to see my next move

I live my life like it's a game of chess

Not monopoly

And even though they claim to see

My next move

They don't see they are playing checkers

Either way, they don't see that my last move

Is better than their next move

Funny how they claim to see my next move

Meanwhile, we are on different games

It's not about who's going to be

The glue to my broken pieces

Because this heart only needs

A band-aid the scar will heal

Even though it doesn't take

An hour

Writer's block

Started from the bottom

Worked my way to the top

From little man

To macho man

My poetry turns winter to spring

Turns summer to fall

I'm a victim of writers' block

Day and night

There's no way to fight it

All I know is

I'm not going to breathe

I'm not going to sleep

I'm not going to eat

I'm going to keep on writing

Until

I see what I want to see

But sometimes I never really

Find the right words to express

How I feel

I feel like my heart is surrounded

By a wall of bricks

I feel like my mind is in a deep hallow pit

So, I sit scribbling everything out

So, I read everything out and

I'm mumbling but I'm

Sitting on my desk trying to

Get the rest of this off my chest

But I can't seem to find it

Like a treasure chest

What we stand for

We don't want to face

The world But

we would rather pace

Ourselves with the materials

Of the world

We don't live on earth anymore

We live in the shadows

We have become more violent but

We still can't fight fear

Are we missing something?

Or maybe we are the ones missing

We always want extra for free

Yet we can't give extra for free

We always complain

But the effort is taken shockingly so plain

I don't know

What do we stand for?

We don't have all the answers

We are all connected

But there's a huge disconnection

Between my culture and yours

Yet we spend money on tours

Trying to learn each other for wars

No matter how the situation is

I don't think we are ever going to

Make it better

Because we have something in common

We are connected by a small thing

We don't know

We don't understand what we stand for

Power

Misuse of power

Can devour

An innocent soul

And turn it into a dark hollow hole

How horrific

How specific it is

To prey on the innocent

Like a hunter hunting on his prey

Using its scent

How its main ability

Is to destroy your sense of morality

Just to benefit your capability

How it draws you away from mankind

And it takes you down like gravity

And it makes you live with depravity

You won't see it because you are blinded by ongoing

Activity

It uplifts you but draws you away from mankind

It devours your availability

It pushes you to your enemies

It puts you around people with negative energies

Misuse of power

Does not only devour

The soul but

It keeps you satisfied

To look for more

It keeps you electrified

With adrenaline

And you spend your time on endless flights

And spend sleepless nights

Eventually, you will live your life like

Bats and owls

But you'll be committing more fouls

It simply draws you away from mankind

It slowly changes your attitude

And no matter the altitude

You will no longer be as kind

And soon enough people will be

Swearing that you are the devil

Because you are beyond blunt

And you are rude on another level

Poetry is Au

Gold, platinum,

Silver, diamonds

And oil

They have it all

Literature, poetry to be specific

Is all I have

It comes from the apex of my heart

No money can buy it

And no money can replicate that apex

If I don't have money, I'm poor

If you don't have poetry, you are empty

They usually say 'poetry is written by those whose

Hearts have been broken'

That's just their slogan

To feed their emptiness

But they don't see that with poetry

All I have is happiness

All the happiness I need

Although I don't look at poetry to make an end need

All I know is I feed

A lot of empty souls and

Heal broken hearts

I see them swimming in pools full of bank notes

From all over the world

But I swim in a room full of poems by poets

From all over the world

They have money, broken souls and lonely hearts

 I have poetry, that heals souls and that's there for

The lonely

They spend their days, spending their money

To fill their emptiness

I spend my days, writing poetry

To heal their hearts

They brag about their money

But behind closed doors

My poems are healing them

Poetry is priceless

Insight

When it comes to literature, poetry has value, not only sentimental value. Poetry has so much value to such a point where people are still reading poems by poets from 16th – 20th century, it [poetry] has so much value to such a point where poets are recognized more than authors and novelists. I mean even the famous writers that we know had a link to poetry, writers such as Sir William Shakespeare, he wrote plays, but he also wrote a few poems, Oscar Wilde known for his novel, 'the picture of Dorian Gray', his novel has a poem written in French.

Schools, libraries and community Centre's teach poetry more than novels, poetry is universal, this means all the languages you can think of have poems written in that language, you don't get novels or plays written in all languages. From any point of view, it's very clear that poetry is very valuable and has a sentimental meaning for every culture there is. I have a theory that people are blinded by things that only give them temporary pleasure, to me, poetry is like a baby and a poet is a mother that's there to nurture that baby, it takes years and years to nurture a baby so as poetry. It takes a long time probably decades to understand yourself as a poet and your purpose and to also understand what message you want to deliver as a poet. It takes decades for these minerals [gold, platinum, diamonds silver, and oil] to be valuable. The earth nurtures these minerals but the only thing different about the earth nurturing minerals and poets nurturing their poems is that minerals deplete, and poems do not. Poetry lives forever longer than the poet there's a lot of poets who have passed but we still enjoy their poems and there are poets being born every day, therefore, poetry never dies.

Why invest in minerals that are going to deplete, why not invest in poetry which lives forever even if the poet dies his/her name will never be forgotten, why are people investing in things they might not live to enjoy. Poetry is priceless, I think it's about time I correct myself, poetry is not Au [gold], Au[gold] has a price tag, which everyone can afford, poetry is from within the heart.

BI LANGUAL

I love Spanish

I love Swahili

I love all eleven of the South African languages

I love Spanish people

I love Dominican people

I love Puerto Rican people

I love Colombian people

I love Latinas

I genuinely love every culture and language

On earth

There's honestly a special way of sexiness

How everyone speaks

How Italians speak, that's nice

Music and Poetry

Music and poetry

Have something in common

The power to express emotion

I'm in love with music

I'm married to poetry

I make music

I don't fake music

I don't hate poetry

Sometimes, frequently

I play music to calm myself

I write poetry to ease my mind

I don't play music to make you

Sick

I write poetry to heal myself

I write poetry to heal you

That's my talent, that's my gift

Music and Poetry have many things

In common

More than what meets the eye

Money or skill

There's nothing more influential than rap music

But everyone claims to know how to use it

But is it money or skill?

Some lack originality

 The truth is heavily pulling them down like gravity

To them, it's all about getting better ratings

Getting paid but they in pains

There's nothing wrong with getting a different

Instrumental

But it's not as if I don't get the sentimental meaning

Why me

I fear that I might end up doing this

For money

I don't want to dumb it down

For money

I'm not a dummy

Either way, I tried to dumb it down

But I wasn't dumb enough

What's this about money or skill

Acceptance

I've always been a poet

But acceptance was the problem

Rhythm and poetry run in my blood

But acceptance was the problem

I didn't fear what society would

Say about me

I still don't fear what society would

Say about me

The world is full of undiscovered poets

What makes me unique from them

But there was one problem,

Acceptance

My greatest fear was recognition

My greatest fear is recognition

I fear that I'll end up writing for fame

I also fear that I wouldn't be recognized

I fear that I might get a little too poetic

I don't want to end up cutting my ear

Like Vincent van Gogh

I've accepted myself

I'm a poet

And I'm poetry in its purest form

War with the minds

I think my mind is in the clouds

No food, no money where are the men of this house

I'm just tired of this systematic oppression

Everyone seems to have depression

This obsession with getting everyone's attention

Lately, everyone is late

I think is about time we get our priorities straight

Lately, we are not there for each other

Lately, we just break each other down

Lately, we live better when someone is under

We seem to live better when someone is under distress

We all seem to be depressed

Black lives matter

No, all lives matter

Don't you see we all work better together?

I'm just exhausted

I'm just tired of this systematic oppression

Put your gun down

This is one war you won't win

Tough talk for a poet though

But that's what you don't know

I don't just come as a poet

I come as an activist

It seems I'm at war with the minds

Clear as diamonds

It seems your emotions were broken down into four letters

On Valentine's day, you sent me a letter

With a simple sentence

"I _ _ _ _ you"

I never got tense in my life like that

Honestly, I was expecting that

I knew we had strong emotions for

Each other

But writing that was crazy

How could you do that

I had doubts

Do you know how many four letter

Words are there

I didn't know which one I had to choose

Do you love me?

Do you hate me?

I know it was valentines and

It's crazy of me to think that you would

Say you hate but

My love, I know you

I know you're crazy enough to tell me

You hate me during valentines

Couldn't you just give me

A box of something

Maybe chocolates or maybe a bike helmet

With your name on it

Why did you go for a letter with that sentence?

That sentence caused stress

But no stress, I love you

I know you love me

Although I didn't know if you love me

I know we just can't stick to simple gestures as

A couple

but can't we just stick to simple gestures next

valentines

is that too much to ask for valentines

I'll save it for Christmas then

Insight

Wow , how this poem came to life was through one of my best friends, Charles , he was dating a friend of ours and she gave him a letter on valentine's day , but this letter was unique, it had 2 words and 4 hyphens basically it was "I---- you" and Charles came to me to help him understand the letter and during that course I noticed that you can actually write "hate" instead of "love" , so the whole experience just stimulated something quite different to me writing poems so that was a good experience, I learned something new and it may have affected how I write poetry.

A letter to my king

I find it hard

I seem to find it hard, why is it hard

For you to express your emotions

In person

It seems that you trust your pen and pad

More than you trust me

I really want to understand you

But I see where I stand

I see what you stand for

I'm trying my best

I'm not implying that you're

A Fool

I just seem to think you're trying to

Make me a fool

It's hard to understand a closed book

Do you understand that I can't always

Wait for you to write another poem

In order for us to talk, I'm your queen

I can tell something is wrong

I can tell from how you hug me that

Your soul is anchored

Your mind is bothered

But I'll always be there day and night

I may not be physically with you but

Itumeleng I'll always be a call way

Pillow talk

From head to toe

She is innocent

And pure as snow

From high to low

Her eyes and smile

Innocence was her flow

There we were the two of us

On the bed

My finger on her forehead

It was midnight

A few hours before the

Morning twilight

The moon was bright

That's the best time for pillow talk

My fingers brushed her hair

And that was the only strike to blow

A cocktail of emotions

Which grow intensely every second

Side to side, side by side

I swear she was my perfect bride

And I was her knight in shining armor

With a shining knightly spear

Whispering into her ear

"I'm here for you,

 I'll protect you, my dear"

With a seductive voice

And her hand on my chest

She pauses and whispers

"when I'm around you I'm lost

In emotions, I can't express how I feel

I'm lost, like being blind in the dark

I'm hard to find, but you're the light

Shining to the rescue"

With her hand on my chest

With the words

"I hope I'm not moving too fast

But I want this to last

I don't want this to be a thing of

The past

I wish I could freeze this moment

And own it"

She continued with her

Angelic voice

I swear if I had a choice

I would only listen to her voice

I was dreaming of our wedding day

Also, our wedding cake

Wedding bells ringing merrily

The golden moment for the galaxy

How I felt like I was lost

Like being blind

in the dark, I'm hard to find

but her voice is there to rescue me

how I felt like we were at the beach

and it was sunset we were taking a walk

but it was all just

pillow talk

A letter to my queen

I find it hard too

To express myself accordingly

I always try but I just don't have

The right words to express how

I feel

I feel like -

I trust you more than anything

I really want you to see that I'm

Also trying

The other night we just clicked

Like magnets, we spent the whole

Night talking, I hope that was a new level

In our relationship

I'm not trying to make you a fool

I feel like the only tool

I need is a pen and pad to express myself

I know it's hard to understand a closed book

That's why I find it easy to sit and cook

A poem, I don't want to confuse you

My soul is beyond being anchored

I can feel it, it's fading, I'm fading

And I try to use all the energy left in me

To express myself as crystal clear as a diamond

Remember I told you I'll get you a diamond

But I see you deserve more than just a diamond

The world is crying

All I hear is people grieving

I hear funeral blues by artists

But against all odds, I pray

I pray to the gods

I pray to the gods that no one

Gets hurt

I think I'm on a mission

To find the missing

Do you get my vision?

Well on the note of visions

I tell visions, I see visions

I see how you see me on

Your televisions but

This is not just any other vision

In this vision, I see your vision too

But what I see

I see the world crying

I see the world crying for help

But no one is there to help

I see the world calling

But no one is answering

I see the world in distress

But no one to the rescue

I see the beginning of the end

Dear Future Mrs.

In life, I have truly longed for someone

Like you

I have truly longed for someone who

I can laugh with

I have truly longed for someone who

I can go crazy with

It's crazy how I have found that someone

It all began with just a smile

That smile was sharper than a sword

That smile had cut me real deep

Deeper than I could describe

Then they didn't want to see us

Together, so they tried to divide

If I were a poet I would not

Choose to write it all to you

I would not need to decide

You would get it all at a blink

Of an eye

I swear it's not a lie

I don't want to sound like a scene

From a romantic movie

But I love you

from here to the moon and back

I don't want to sound cliché

But I would die for you

Count your blessings

I wonder if you know

How special you are

I wonder if you know

How precious you are

I wonder if you know

How lucky I am to have you

In my life but I seem-

I seem to wonder if you know

How blessed you are to have

Me in your life I seem –

To wonder if you know

How rare I am

I see to wonder if you know

I seem to wonder if you know

How gifted you are

I seem to wonder if you know

How privileged you are

I seem to wonder if you know

I seem to wonder if you know

The meaning of all the roses I give you

I seem to wonder if you are

Counting your blessings

Insight

Each color of a rose has a meaning, it symbolizes something. Red roses symbolize love, yellow roses symbolize friendship, dark pink roses symbolize gratitude, orange roses symbolize desire, not lust, peach roses symbolize appreciation and just as common as the red roses the white roses symbolize purity.

So, halfway through the first part of the book and I fall victim to writer's block, the worst case of writer's block although I wasn't expecting to fall victim at the early stages of the writing this book, I had prepared for it. The timing was off by many months, the scary part is that I was home for holidays, but it was a huge advantage for me mainly because I had a proper chance to roam around looking for the "fuel for my brain", you know, some inspiration.

The weather was perfect, I had all the time and the only thing I prescribed for such cases was to call my best friends, Patrick, Chantel, Olerato, and Junior. I knew they were the ones to hit some inspiration into my head, did it work? That's the only question I still ask myself but that's only for you to find out. At this stage, I had not told anyone including my best friends that I'm writing a book.

Yes, they knew I'm a poet, they knew I wrote poetry, they didn't know I was attempting to write a book. Keeping such a secret was a push factor to making sure I complete the first part of the book in the required time. Well I don't rush, and I didn't rush my work, but I had given myself enough time to complete my first book at a specific time frame [2 years], but my goal was completing the book in 2 years so that was automatically my motivation.

Honestly , writing the first part of the book so far had been quite a blast, I enjoyed , the emotions are genuine which was mainly the 'motto' for this book "keeping it 1000% real, keeping it 1000% honest" so I was glad that I had been able to express my saddest, angriest, happiest and all those emotions properly from my heart through the pen to the notepad . I think it showed all those moments you would think I'm going crazy or something , although I must say during the writing of the first part of this book I learned that I was a little bit in my own universe or planet, [I think I would call it planet E-901], which in a certain way had an influence in the next part of this book ,but I'm not going to spoil it for you.

Constant shifts

What's the cause of these decisions?

Living,

In a world where schools are built to be prisons

In a world where nothing stays the same

Living

In a world where everyone's hungry

But no, we don't stay the same

Living In a jungle full of concrete

And lately, everyone's trying to compete

Lately, everyone's telling a lie

Lately, everyone's full of hate

Lately, everyone's late

Everyone's around me but no one can relate

Every night

I gaze into the sky

The stars are telling me to fight

For everything to be alright

I might fight for what's right

But I feel like

I might not be doing the most

I feel like

I might be a ghost in society

I feel like

I know society is suffering from anxiety

Welcome to *Planet E901*

Part 2

this part has thirty-three poems

1. Universe
2. Alienated
3. Gia visto [déjà vu]
4. Madi a segosi! [Royal blood]
5. These Thoughts
6. Mi Amor [my love]
7. Lost in my thoughts
8. Stacey
9. A wise owl once whispered
10. Mafia persona
11. Pain [she is pain]
12. Control
13. Pain [she was in pain]
14. Initial meaning
15. Significant other
16. first love
17. I Don't feel creative
18. Fade away
19. New lab rat
20. I hope I didn't fail you
21. It's time to rise to my feet
22. Not anymore
23. Mine
24. Clear skies no moon
25. An open letter
26. Meditation
27. All in a word
28. Day in, day out
29. The silence is too loud
30. HD vision
31. Limitless
32. Streets of the city of gold
33. Galaxies collide

Hello again, now this might be a little too interesting for you , I still question myself about the meaning, purpose, and role of a poet in society and I noticed through research that most poets don't usually write thought-provoking poems, which I found really not fair because there are certain thought-provoking things which are happening around us and we are not expressing or rather discussing those issues but I don't blame poets. I'm under the impression that you, the audience, the readers, the fans are not demanding thought-provoking content, so as a "dash" of uniqueness I decided that I'm going to evoke creativity and imagination as much as I can , so I decided that it's about time you get to see what's really going on in my brain and also thought that it's time we both take poetry to a level where poetry has never been to , so if you are active on social media just hashtag #ON_A_DIFFERENT_LEVEL when you do or post anything that's creative or send an email of your creative poems or thoughts to tmlngkekana@gmail.com with the subject 'poetry on a different level' . LET_POETRY_BE_HEARD.

So back to the current book, you're about to enter the heart of the book and the following chapter is a very evoking chapter in this book because it's all about letting the audience understand the real message or the message behind the descriptive lines and rhymes of the poet without misunderstanding or losing the whole point of the poem, buckle up this is about to get crazy, expect the unexpected.

Just for clarification purposes, the previous page is basically a 'table of contents' for this coming Chapter, chapter 2.

Universe

I'm on a verge right now

To turn the meaning of poetry up-side-down

So that I can give you more than this verse

So that I can give you the universe

So that I can give you the moons and stars

Because there's no love like that

I'm on a verge right now

To turn the meaning of poetry up-side-down

So that you can give it to me so complicated

Without contemplating

So that I can give it to you so simple

With a crocodile smile

Probably with a dimple

I'm on a verge right now

To turn the meaning of poetry up-side-down

So that I can give you all the galaxies

So that I can give you all my melodies

Because my melodies are remedies

I'm on a verge right now

To turn the meaning of poetry up-side-down

For you

Because you are the center of my universe

Alienated

Lately, I don't feel the same

All I ever do is sit with a pen

And paper and dig through my thoughts

Not looking for gold

Not looking for a reason to be negative

But looking for golden memories

Looking for the truth

Looking for happiness

I'm looking for positivity

that's my main activity

Do I try too much?

Am I pushing a little too much?

Is it wrong to be a little bit too much?

But_

Am I going crazy?

Maybe I'm just looking in the wrong place

Maybe I should be looking in my heart

Maybe_

I just feel so alienated

Due to reasons that I am highly diverse and I love learning new things, I came to a decision after an intriguing conversation with my cousin (Frank Sediko). I decided to dedicate the second part of this book to all the languages I can be able to learn, I had to learn as many languages as I could, which as a result introduced me to many people, some we met online and some we shared the same interests such as learning different languages , Frank , obviously helped with translating some of my poetry.

'Gia visto' [Déjà vu] is a diverse poem, which is made up of 4 languages [French, Portuguese, Spanish, Swahili],'gia visto' when translated, it basically means 'Already seen', which is basically [déjà vu]. The idea behind this versatile poem was to show unity but it was one of my many odd ways of introducing you to a creative, diverse, versatile part of this book. I mean, honestly, I did warn you that this part of the book is "the heart of this book" which is about to get unique from the other parts of the book.

It's my utmost pleasure to welcome you to the extreme part of this book, but it's not only the extreme part of my book, but it also symbolizes my character, to make things a little convenient for you and me, below every poem shall be a standard English version of that poem

Enjoy.

Gia Visto [déjà vu]

Me paro frente a una multitud

tan humilde como puedo ser

pero todos me miran como si

estuvieran protagonizado las nubes

Suis-je prêt à recite ma poésie

Suis-je prêt à laisser les gens

Entrer dans mon Cœur

Je viens d`avoir faim

Je me sens comme dans le jardin d'Eden

Entoure d`un tas d`Eve

sio tu hadithi ya kuwaambia ukwelia

lakini nadhani itakuwa bora kama

wewe kujiweka katika nafasi yangu

kuchukua hatua katika viatu

vyangu na kutembea

talvez voce entenda

Eu sinto que estou preso en minha mente

Eu sinto que estou expressando uma mentira

Mas limpe as nao chore

E solo un déjà vu

[Déjà vu]

(Translated)

I stand in front of a crowd

As humble as I can ever be

But they all stare at me

As if they are staring into the clouds

Am I ready to recite my poetry?

Am I ready to let people into

My life?

I'm just hungry I feel like

I'm in the garden of Eden

Surrounded by a bunch of eves'

I'm not just storytelling

I'm telling the truth

But I think it would be better

If you put yourself in my position

Take a step into my shoes and

Walk

Maybe you will understand

I feel like I'm trapped in my own mind

I feel like I'm expressing a lie

But wipe off the tears, don't cry

It's Just déjà vu

Madi a segosi

Ke wa madi a segosi

Mme ke phela bophelo

Jo bo tshetlha bo le swadi

Bogosi bo taboga mading

Bo jetswe mo teng gaaka

Jaaka dithito tsa setlhare

Dinwelelang teng tlase ga mmu

Jaaka thipa ya botoro

Kgolong ka boko jo bo

Lweditsweng

Mme ke se ke kopane le mantswe

A go tlhalosa, ka se ke kgone

Tlhagisa tlhaloso sentle mme ke sala

Ka tshobostsi le semelo

Kgolong ya bogosi

Dula ka gangwe

Moeteledipele wa kgotla yaaka

Gonne ka kakaretso ya sotlhe

Nka tswa ke tshela jaaka thipa ya botoro

Mme morago ke sa le ka

madi a segosi

[Royal Blood]

(madi a segosi translated)

I am of royal blood

But I live my life

As plain and blunt

As a butter knife

Royalty flowing in my veins

Rooted within me like

A tree's roots

Sipping deep into the soil

Raised with a sharpened mind

But I can't find

The right words to explain

And yet

And yet, all I'm trying to do is

Regain

And maintain my mainframe

To be at once, the leader

Of my kingdom

Because after all

I may live like a butter knife but

I am of royal blood

Insights

When I wrote this poem, I was (in Mahikeng, north west province) and I think what sort of inspired this poem, was the idea that I was home and I believe my heart at this point was at its peaceful state which allowed me to get wildly creative. This allowed me to connect with my inner being, to tap into my consciousness, to connect with my soul, this honestly got the most of me, I mean I was at a point where I could write poetry without being bothered, without being interrupted.

I wrote royal blood due to the stories my grandmother told me, that we are from a royal family, as old as I am, I was sceptical when she told me that we are royalty but as she presented evidence that we are royal, I was excited.

Basically, this poem was to show that even though I didn't grow up in a castle with a throne and guards, but at the end of the day I grew up with royalty flowing in my veins. That maybe, possibly, I'm a blessing in disguise.

It's a powerful poem, but it's very clear, there is no double meaning behind this poem, you know, it's straight forward. This poem says a lot, even though I felt like writing more, I felt like what I wrote was enough to get the message through.

I'm very diverse and bi-lingual, but my Setswana is not 1000%, so my poem was happily and willingly translated by my cousin, Frank Sediko. He was quite impressed by the poetic content, the message of the poem as he was translating, I mean from one poet to another, I think from that point onwards he was in sync with me, you know, it was easier for him to connect with my other poems and to understand how I live.

Which was the main point, the main goal of the book, to connect the reader with the poem because once that's achieved, then automatically the reader has connected with me (the poet). Therefore, I felt like I was already achieving the goal, you know, slowly but surely achieving the goal.

These Thoughts

Are you happy or sad?

We live in a world that

You are either good or bad

I'm not trying to make you

Mad or angry

Matter of fact you should,

Thank me

That I'm basically educating you

About the real and the fake

That I'm basically liberating you

Honestly, that's great

You should just compose yourself

And get rid of the hate

Wait

Fame is a dangerous game

In that game, people don't stay the same

Mind your space

Take it slow and mind your pace

Mi Amor
[my love]

I don't think you know how much

It means to feel your tender touch

I see a burst of lust in your eyes

It's intoxicating my mind

How I wish you were mine

You don't know but I'm losing mind

Seeing you is like

Seeing the sunset lighting up

A portion of the sky before

It would retire to its bed and

Let the moon start its reign

Lost in my thoughts

A glance into your eyes and I am lost
in time and space

With just a glance, I'm lost in my thoughts

I start seeing us
every time I see you

And when

I'm with you

Everything freezes

You are always breathtaking

I don't know...

Well...

I can't recall but

One thing I'm certain of is that

We were meant to be

STACY

She looks lonely

Her poems are filled

With sorrow and

Nothing but bitter tears

She's (EXTREMELY BEAUTIFUL)

She's lava, she melts hearts

I see a faint reflection

Of myself in her eyes

I see her love in the

Night skies

Her peaceful smile

Is as sharp as a sword

It cuts deep into my heart

And yet

I still envy how

She's mysterious and unpredictable

She wrote to me that

She envy's how

I'm mysterious and unpredictable

Insight

Stacy is a girl who is very blunt and rude but she has the biggest heart and is always real. She's funny, cute and sometimes goofy, she will try to make you laugh when you're sad she'll always try to be a shoulder to cry on, she always puts others before herself. She has been hurt all her life, so when she tells you she loves you she means it. She is very weird and passionate about others. A shy girl in the beginning but as you get to know her, you learn that she's quite the opposite of shy, she's loud, she's beautiful, she's loyal and she's dangerous, not a person to hurt.

A Wise owl once whispered

A wise owl once whispered

I have emotions

As big as oceans

I have thoughts

As deep as oceans

But yet you don't see me

Cause commotions

I'm a wise owl

I'm not doing this for fame

I'm as real as they come

Don't play this is not a game

Mafia Persona

I'm an arsenic writer

Don't you play with me

I'm not your friend,

I'm your enemy

Be careful

I'm not just your regular entity

I just don't like your negative energy

Sorry, I don't know what got into me

I no longer have that sympathy

So, you're a poet with a gun

What's the matter?

What happened to

Your pen being your dagger

So, you're trying to use me to get up the ladder

But it seems things aren't getting better

A story of a mob boss

Pain
[she is pain]

How can she ease the pains?

When she feels like she's locked up in chains

How can she ease the pain?

When she feels like she's trapped in her own brain

How can she ease the pain?

If she can't explain

How she feels

How can she ease the pain?

When she clearly doesn't know

She looks lonely and

Her eyes are filled with sorrow

Her are filled with sour tears

She tries to put a beautiful smile but

How can she ease the pain?

When she is clearly

In Pain

Control

I feel like I'm losing control

I feel like I'm losing the plot

Oh why, do I feel this way

Oh why, do I think this way

Is everything going to be okay?

I'm there for you, I'll be there for you

The lethal words we use as we claim

To support but you don't know

You have not felt the pain

Of seeing a teenage boy/girl hung with a gold chain

These children live a sad life

These children die in a sad way

These children die in silence

Yet We ask ourselves where the get their violence

Seems like not everyone has control

Seems like there's no

Control

Pain

[she was in pain]

I wake up every morning
To a call "without you, I'd still be
In pain, I'd still be in mourning"

"you and I have that connection
It's more of a chemical reaction
You are my distraction
You take my pain away
Every single earth day"

"I wonder if I'll ever discover
A passion like you and
I wonder if I'll ever recover the life I had"

"you actually never judged my past
Even though
I was too fast to judge you
Who knew after looking up into the skies?
I was already looking at you
A blessing in disguise"

She was in pain
She vowed she'll never die in vain

Initial meaning

The Initial purpose of writing poetry

Was to vent, I wrote my problems away

And after writing I'd feel okay

The initial purpose of writing poetry

Was to impress girls

A couple of words

A couple of rhymes

A couple of, "roses are red

Violets are blue"

I swear you'd also think the love is true

That was the initial purpose but now

I write poetry to my utmost honesty

To honestly express my emotions

The whole deal

Is to be real

The whole deal

Is to heal

Significant other

I can never hold you down

All I can ever do is lift you up

Like the crown you wear

Like the crown you are

You are beautiful without knowing it

A sweet perfumed rose in whose petals

Cupid lurks in ambush

Every time I'm with you

I feel like checking in at the

Universal space station, probably for a vacation

On Venus

Like cupid

You are only part human

But you're not really like Cupid

You are Aphrodite

Love, beauty, pleasure, and procreation

Highly intelligent

You truly deserve those qualities

You also deserve to get

Myrtles, Roses, Doves, Sparrows, and swans

Every single day

For every single breath, you take

My Significant other

Insight

I believe love can't be described in words, no matter how many adjectives you are capable of using. Love can only be felt and so is the beautiful moments between the two people deeply in love.

Love is not about the expensive gifts, or the matching outfits or the relationship goals posts and photos...love is about those tiny gestures, you know... holding hands, cuddling, kissing , or the sweet poem from your significant other(a good way to show your loved one he/she means a lot, hint hint) ,the sweet genuine loving compliments, along with the "I'll always be your shoulder to cry on" moments, or the " let's play video games, or board games" moments, or the simple " let's stay in and watch some movies or a series together" moments. It's really honestly about the little things that you do that matters the most, the tiny gestures take a relationship far, they increase the trust within the relationship.

First love

My darling I wrote you another letter

I heard you aren't well; I hope you get better

I know you don't probably hear this every day

But everything is going to be okay

What I'm about to say might sound sketchy

Girl, I love you

I love the sound of that, it sounds catchy

It's so sad, you don't know that-

Don't get mad but I'm your number 1 fan

Man, it's not a lie, no it's not a scam

My darling here's another letter

Just wanted to tell you

You looked beautiful in that sweater

Honestly, it doesn't matter

You still look beautiful, with or without that sweater

To more serious matters

It really shatters my heart

That we really fell apart

You dwell deep within my heart

I don't think I've told you this, but

Your beauty and intelligence are truly a work of art

My dear, honestly, I don't like your negligence

It's fine though If you really don't want to talk to me

I've said my heart out, I've opened my chest

And 500 words came from my heart

500 words on how much I love you

I thought the truth sets you free but

I'm going to let you be

I hope you can also open your chest

I hope...be my guest

I guess this is my last letter

To you

You will always be in the center of my heart

Always,

Your love

I Don't feel creative

Dear brain, it's now been two months

I'm really tired of these stunts

You know everybody wants to flow like me

But suddenly

I can't even write poetry

Now, I don't feel creative

I guess it's a sign or

More of a lesson that I should be more appreciative

And to adore

Nature

Fade away
[Fading away]

Fade away

I'm fading away

My heart is aching all day

I'm being pulled into a dark hole

Knee deep into the sand, I can't even walk

I can feel an anchor on my soul

That's how I feel when I miss you

☐

New lab rat

There's a new breed

Holding the pen differently

Please, try to understand me

Because I don't really understand

These poets

New emotions with a touch of

The 70's poetry

Are we trapped in the same system?

As the poet's in the '70s

Love, war, we're just looking for peace

We're looking for peace

But there's no peace in the mind

Something we're all trying to find

We're all looking for peace

We're all trying to be kind

New lab rats

I hope I didn't fail you

I hope you are not aggravated

I'm just highly motivated

I'm speechless

Where do I begin

I hope everything is still good

Between ...

... us ...

It's time to rise to my feet

I guess it's time to make amends

To those who I may have hurt

I guess it's time to pace

Myself

This is not a game

This is My own life,

My own race

I have no choice, I have to embrace

I guess it's time to fly

Like a dragonfly

Sting like a box jellyfish

Not anymore

Not anymore

This is it

This is where I draw the line

I think it's about time

To free my mind

And speak my heart out

Mine

A woman once said, boy what's your name

What you are doing is good, just stay in your own lane

The conversation with the woman was amusing

I found it a little confusing

I said

In the beginning I felt like my heart was stone cold

Although now I feel like it's made of gold

I waited for everything to unfold

She said

It's scary right, is it not?

Waiting for time to heal you, while your life is tangled in a knot

Waiting for everything to pan out, while the pot gets hot

I felt like she read my mind

Then she said something that blew my mind

She said, you thought you were a lost soul but

All you had to do is find

The right flow

Something that kept you one of a kind

Well we are left with only 10 poems then we are officially done with the unclear, unstable emotions. For clarification, I'm not depressed, I have been questioned whether I'm going through some depressive stage, no I'm not.

Anyways, as I said we are only left with 10 poems then we are done with chapter 2 (planet e901), this has been quite a rollercoaster, my life is a big rollercoaster. I hope I have taught you a few things, more especially that, you know there were different languages in this chapter.

Honestly, chapter 2 has been that part of the book where a deeper connection was made, in terms of communication and understanding you.

chapter 3 (being one with nature) is quite different from [the beginning of a new journey] and [planet e901], this chapter is really about being one with nature, but I do not want to focus on it a lot. The right time to talk about it will come, enjoy these last 10 poems and I will catch you on the next and last chapter of this book.

Clear skies no moon

The sky is so clear

The stars are twinkling

I'm sitting on my chair

Wondering

Wondering if

Maybe I'm drifting

Maybe I'll see my flaws

Maybe I'll see what I'm seeking

I'm intrigued

What am I staring at?

Am I staring into a place?

Above and beyond

A place no living thing can replace

Am I staring into someone's face?

The sky is clear

There's no moon but

I bring brightness to the darkness

That reigns

Galaxies collide

Worlds collide

The universe slowly shifts

Planets are rearranged

Two galaxies drift

And collide

That's how we met

It's not a coincidence

It was destiny

It was meant to be

It was not for us to decide

Even though it doesn't have to be clarified

Maybe we are each other's blessings in disguise

Maybe we are each other's gifts

That's why we exchanged

Paths, I bet it was set

To happen and yet

We act as if it's an incident

As if it's a test to our innocence because

We live freely

We don't live an abstemious way of

Life

An open letter

To the Moon
The wolves will cry

To the universe
The galaxies will collide

To the Kings and Queens
An heir will be born

To the pyramids in Egypt
The stars will align

To you
I shall always find peace
I shall always confine in you

Meditation

I am one with the mind

In a state where

I see through my mind's eye

A state so rare

A state far from negativity

A state of tranquility

A state beyond

All In a word

A word that motivates

A word that educates

A word that can make

Or break

A word not known

A word, never used

It all started with a word and

All that can be said

Can be said in a word

Day in, day out

Everyday

Day in, day out

We meet all kinds of people

We face our greatest fears

We face the toughest trials

But

We are strong, we'll be okay

Day in, day out

We walk through the face of the world

With tears held back

With a smile and a great goal

In mind

Because

Whatever that doesn't break you

Makes you stronger

But

If you can no longer cope

Don't lose hope

I'll always be a shoulder to cry on

A pillar of support

The silence is too loud

When silence overcomes me
my thoughts makes the loudest noises

Yet
when there's no silence

My thoughts still make the loudest noises
I keep wondering

I keep questioning myself
am I supposed to see everything

In a poetic way
am I normal?

HD vision

Black bike

Black jeans

Black boots

Black helmet

All matte black

Tattoos all over my body

Riding until there's nowhere

To ride to

Free at last

Feeling the wind brush through

My hair

It's my Harley Davidson

It's my HD vision

Limitless

When you create
Something beautiful
Do you ever think?

When you create
Something beautiful
You just dream

You believe

When you create
Something beautiful
You explore, then

Discover something beautiful

Something beautiful
Comes from being
Limitless

If being limitless
Brings so much beauty
Why do we live so limited

Why can't we live our lives limitless
Why can't we live like that everyday
Every second

Why can't we be
Limitless

The capital city

Everyone is here

this is where money is made

the streets are filled with purpose

Art is everywhere

in every wall

in every corner

From the Union Buildings

to the South African Reserve Bank

from Freedom Park

to the State Theatre

It may not be the 'City of Gold'

but it's the capital city of South Africa

A city where history lives and breathes

a city where the streets speak

a city where memories are made

a city where that ignites excellence

this is not just a city in south Africa

this is

the capital city of South Africa

Being one with nature

Chapter 3

1. The son of the soil
2. End of your reign
3. By Your Side
4. Fire
5. Put down the pen
6. Therapeutic
7. She is a purple flower
8. Cool breeze
9. Aura
10. Winter
11. I'm something rare
12. Beyond what meets the eye
13. Roses
14. Dreamy place
15. Having to be original {H_2O}
16. Eruptive Volcano
17. Worth
18. Balances
19. What happened that night
20. It's time to fly
21. Still alive
22. Here goes gravity
23. Jungle
24. My symbol
25. Young king
26. Are we all alone?
27. I thought about it
28. If it's a mix up
29. It's never too late
30. Regrets
31. Invocation
32. Bee leave
33. What's death

The son of soil

Sun for soil
Energy for ground
Family to be proud

Son for soul
Son for soil

For so God loved the world that
he gave his only beloved son

Emerged from dust to flesh by
the word of the creator

Son of soil

I'm the son of South
The Son of soil
Soil of Earth
Ground of God

I'm the seed that was planted
before the Egyptians discovered the pyramids
planted in front of Philippians but could not
be found
I'm the son of soil
I'm an African son that skipped
predicted calculations of scientists
in order to accumulate and
exterminate the world civilization

I'm that Sun that burn the lines of
Latitude and Longitude
Reconstruct lines of orbits and their
attitude
The same son that escaped the spell of
bad gratitude and multitude
The son of Khoi in the circle of the fourth generation

For the sun that goes up and down
again
serving the purpose of the creator
not blaming the glucose of nature
The son that's living in the film of lecture

The son of soil

I'm the son of soil
The sun for soul

The son of soil

End of your reign

As it rains

What a gloomy day

But there's no other way

To say this

It's the end of your reign

What's a King without a Queen?

No need to fear

I'm the new king

By Your Side

I'm on another level

Maybe I'm lying

Is it me or is it you?

Am I holding you down?

Are you holding me down?

I just want to spread my wings

And you just want to fly

All the we been through

I don't want go through it twice

All alone

I know it feels like

You are all by yourself but

I'm always by your side

Fire

I feel like someone just lit

Fire inside of me

The insanity

Well in my mind I am fire

My soul is the lighter

My poetry is the spark

I simply get things lit up

Put the pen down

Lately they rely in loud music

To express themselves

Lately all they want to do is music

They don't even know the purpose

Of music

They really want to do it but they can't

There's no way to copy creativity

I think it's time to put the pen down

Therapeutic

Modern life is too abusive
it's quite elusive

Pen slowly meets paper
no need to rush, no need to caper

Once upon a time

Beyond time
there was a boy
he didn't work a 9 to 5
but more of a 365 for life

The constant battles with his mind
the pain was equivalent to
1000 needles slowly striking the skin

But he had joker's grin on his face
an odd place
it seems

A purple flower

She is a flower
She is rain

She is a flower that maintains its color
during the seasonal changes

A flower with the power
to attract all kinds of butterflies
and bees

She is the only flower
That brightens my day even
on a gloomy day

And Yet

She is not only a flower

She is rain
She is, Purple rain

Rain that relieve the drought
rain that brings joy and
when I walk through the scorching hot valley
she is the rain
that quenches the thirst of a nation
she is the reason for a beautiful rainbow

she is,
Purple Rain

she is,
A Purple Flower

Cool Breeze

I feel the cool breeze

Through my hair

I get a chill

Through my back

It's quite cold

It's freezing cold

Aura

Be careful
my mind is racing
my intuition slowly pacing
just be careful of who you are facing

I don't really know
am I lost in my own thoughts
is this really how it goes

I see your aura
so colorful
I see how the planets are aligned
I see how troubled mankind is

I seem to be trapped
between the past, present and future
trapped in the moment

Winter

Oh winter
the trees are lonely
the days are filled with the same color

Boring

Even though you come with gifts
it seems the birds aren't happy
about your visit and have
decided to move to the north

It seems the grizzlies aren't happy
as they have decided to sleep until
you leave

Oh Winter

Oh Winter

Oh why

Dear Winter

I'm something rare

When you are in a place of tranquillity
they will look at you like you are a mad person
because I once told them
I thought I was walking through a valley but
clearly, I was walking through a dragon's belly

So typical but
let's not get stereotypical
we are all born to die
it's not biblical

Sometimes
I always feel like I'm frozen in time
but sometimes I feel like optimus prime
I wish I could not use a rhyme but
I can feel it
that I'm on my prime
that it's time

To expand
to show you where I stand
to make you understand
I would like to explain but
I might go insane
even though sometimes
this gift to write poetry
feels like a curse
I'm happy because
poetry is flowing deep inside my blood
I know that this is destiny

Beyond what meets the eye

One day I'll be a nobody, **you will** not even **remember me**
You will not even **miss me**, if I'm lucky you will only have faint
memories of me
sometimes – not **often**, you will see me in public and
you will quietly say to yourself
' that guy looks familiar'

It's all about time though...
One day to someone I will not be just a 'person'
to that person **everything** they see and touch or smell **will**
bring back fond memories of us
that person won't spend a day without annoyingly saying
they miss me

To that person **everything we have done and** everything
we have **been through** will be a reassurance that tomorrow
there's still something to look forward to **and**
as time goes on, the more we'll be excited for the adventures
waiting for us

It will be **a** long life **friendship,** one that lives for decades
one that lives to see generations after us but
to you I **will only be a memory**
A " once upon a time" **story** that doesn't end
with a "happily ever after" but unfortunately it will be too late for you

With time
A relationship would have grown and matured
Like wine
The older it is, the **sweet**er it tastes
a statement that contradicts that**,** all
old things are **sour and** outdated
the beauty of life in more than a nutshell

Something that cannot be seen because
its **beyond what** the eyes can see
beyond what **meets the eye**

Roses

You are my rose

You are beautiful

No matter the time of day

You are strong

You are caring

You are patient

You take your time

And you need all the care you get

A dreamy place

I dream
I dream of better days
I dream of a better place
like the long walk to freedom but
it was a dream that came to reality

I dream
I dream of calling you, mine
I dream of my success falling
my reputation tumbling but
for you I don't mind

My hopes are high but
my dreams are brighter

I dream
I dream of happiness
not my happiness, your happiness
I dream of a long prosperous journey
with you

I dream
I dream of a place
a place where there's us
a place for us
a dreamy place

Having to be original
{ H2O }

From the margins

From one paragraph to the other

From one sentence to the next

From a single letter

The written words have a better meaning

Every written word has a true meaning

Perhaps writing down how you feel

You might just realise how real it is

How crucial it is to be original

Eruptive volcanoes

Somewhere in the world there's
A young female who is constantly molested by her father
he is supposed to protect her
he is just a wolf in a sheep's clothing
now she is exploding with self-loathing
all hunched over in the corner of her room
her hands on her head, touch knees and elbows
she is in pain
she starts yelling until her lungs start failing
nobody is there to keep her mellow

She turns to music; she channels her pain into her mic
she holds her mic like she is going to asphyxiate it
the tunes keep playing and she sings her lungs
like a volcano her emotions erupt

On the other side of the world there's
a young weeping fellow
his head on the pillow
he can't sleep, he is in pain
he bellows
nobody is there to keep him mellow
so he turns to music,
he channels his pain through his cello
like volcano
he erupts, emotions just flow
he is in the dark but he glows

Worth

I know what you want

I know you want me

You want me to show you off

I know

I know you know your worth

I just don't know

I don't know if I'm worthy

Balances

Every word I scribble

Reflects the truth

The good and the bad

Of everything around me

But...

...it's not just any story, it's life

It is a way of life

it's a balance

like Yin Yang

What happened that night

It was like time had paused

As if the stars were aligned

The night was alive

If you were quiet enough,

You could hear it breathe

The energy was unique

Something quite rare but

It seemed like it was all normal

It seemed like I was the only one experiencing

Something new

The night sky was very beautiful

It was like the universe was expressing itself

To me,

To the world

What happened that night was

Quite an adventure, a blessing

It was the night of an eclipse

The Luna eclipses

It's time to fly

Ten toes on the ground

I guess it's time to

Prepare my wings to fly

Because it's time for me

To fly

Fly high

Still alive

Once met a drunk man he said to me
oh why am I like this
oh why am I feeling this way
oh why am I thinking like this
I don't think you understand kid
let's take a breather

We sat down and said
I really want you to understand this
don't be ignorant, ignorance is bliss
like Adam and Eve the big man
breathed life into me but
I was young, wild, stupid
I stuck a knife into me
like I had a life to give

once took a gun fully loaded and
I stuck a bullet into me
I guess it wasn't meant to be
I don't feel any more
I don't feel pain, pleasure or sympathy
I'm such a loser , I can't even be sober for a day
kid look at me ,
I'm even embarrassed to say you must look at me
take my advice be real to yourself that's the only way
to keep your sanity

Here goes gravity

Where do I begin?

To the life of young boy indie

He has the mic on his hand,

He's backstage he can see the crowd

His audience, 20 000 people

He realizes it's time to recite the poems

he has been scribbling down

but he's nervous, he's sweaty

he knows that he's ready

he takes a step to the spotlight

and he whispers to himself

"here goes gravity"

He recites his poem with melody

Nobody realizes he's talking about his own life

About reality

As he finishes with his poem

The audience loves him,

They are throwing roses at his feet

But he's only looking at one person

With a smile on his face,

He takes his final bow and

The big red curtains close

Jungle

A place,
beyond my wildest dreams
to build my movement
I hope it doesn't lead to my descend
to build my legacy

A place,
A modern jungle
full of concrete
where everyone is trying to compete
with one another, with one goal and
you can't concede
a place to plant your own seed

A place,
filled with crooked minds
very similar to a war zone
I try to
I hope I find my own zone
far from violence
I try to
I hope I can call it my own home

Once a place of tranquillity but
now a place we have to fight for equality
a place far from harmony but
I pray every day that we all find that one melody
our melody
I pray every day that we can all embrace that mentality

My Symbol

This is my symbol of

Love

This is my symbol of

Hope

This is my symbol of

Support

This is my symbol of

Safety

For growth

Young king

Every time I think of people like

Kendrick Lamar, J Cole,

Oprah Winfrey, Ellen Degeneres

Dr Phil

I think of people who are real

I think of people like me

People who spread love and peace so heavily

To be honest there's no need to be a celebrity

It just flows like a melody

As I browse through my memory

I notice that I'm talking about royalty

And I'm just a

Young king

Are we all alone?

It seemed like an ordinary day

A little too ordinary I may say

Even though everything looked in place

Something was out of its way

As I was taking a walk,

Something caught my attention

What if –

What if aliens came and invaded this planet?

Would they go around disintegrating everyone

Would we even be able to fight for ourselves?

Are we even prepared for such things?

Even though there are infinite galaxies

This planet can't be the only planet in the universe

With life

Are we all alone, I doubt so?

I thought about it

So, I thought –

I thought back to reality

I thought about my insanity

I thought –

How you keep me sane

How you never keep it plain

How you always say there's nothing to lose

But something to gain

So, I thought to myself

How do you keep it so real?

How do you live life so fulfilled?

Is it all a dream?

Do you get what I mean?

I thought about it

If it's a mix up

I wonder

If it's a mix up

This is beyond the lines of life

This is, the lines of life

Maybe it was too good to be true

You were the only one I knew

So how could this be mix up

I wonder

If it's a mix up

It's never too late

If you are reading this

It's never too late

To determine your own fate

It's never too late

To take your position

To sit on your throne

Of your precious land

It's never too late

I know you have been longing

To know where you come from

Where you belong

It's been a long time but

It's never too late

Regrets

What's a King without a Queen?

If it was not about love

Honestly

We won't be looking above

But

My only regret

Is not loving you enough

My only regret is that

I was too young for you

And you were too young for me

Invocation

I silently kept my talent vexed

Lately everyone wants to be the GOAT

I just want to be a T-REX

The Realest E...

Should I finish the rest

So as

I search for my blessings

I pray for my enemies

The real and fake

That they throw the hate in the lake

Lately

I have been doing what I please

So, I decided, I looked at my soul

Straight in the eyes

 Then I realised

I fear naught but God

Bee leave

I close my eyes

And hold my breath

I made a wish

I wished

I wished to have a personality of a bee

That I could believe

More in myself

What's death?

A dark cloud that brings joy
there's no life without death
just as there's no death without life

Someday, sooner or later
a journey ends and a new one begins
someday, my home will be filled with family,
friends, church members and the community
a time in life where the funeral blues are
played – sung
a time where a life is truly celebrated
not a time to be sad
unfortunately not in my conscious presence
because I'll be a peaceful place

Right?

As my corpse lay peacefully in a comfortable casket
my loved ones , my family , my friends , everyone
will be forced to bid me goodbye
    " 'till we meet again"
everyone will be forced to keep it one thousand
just as I kept it one thousand
to my friends , all the good memories will start to
play and
all of a sudden , all the little things I did will
remind them of me

Right?

A brief summary of my life will be given
somehow it will be highly filtered
not how I would present it
during the final stretch of my physical
presence , the funeral blues will get
louder and tears will flow the pastor will say
" from dust we were made to dust we shall return"
" from ashes to ashes" "from soil to soil" and

my coffin will be slowly put down
six feet deep

What's death
death is a gift
to meet all the angels and saints
to meet God
"we were all born to die"
to live for eternity
death was never about pain
death is all about peace

Right?

What's death?

Bonus poems

1. Appreciate
2. Poetry 101 [food for the soul and heart]

Appreciate

From time to time

From rhyme to rhyme

They try to break me but I'm on my prime

This is just the beginning of my story

Poetry flows deep in my circulatory

System

A wise owl will whisper into your ear

It's about time you appreciate him

Poetry 101
Food for the soul and heart

What's life, life is too short and
The youth is just sniffing their lives away
Sometimes it's hard to see that
Somethings are timeless even though
We are the future of the past,
We are the present, so we know
What's wrong and right, sometimes
We just need a number one fan but
One problem about Us is that
We want to be all alone
It should be Us against the world but
What's different about Us, is that
we glow , it's not rare anymore to
Have the brightest star in the universe standing
right in front of you

Sometimes it's all about time
Sometimes you just have to do it
It doesn't need to take a hundred years
A century, to decide
sometimes it's hard to realise that
This generation is a different breed
Sometimes we don't realise that
Good things take time
Like 9 months , like September
Sometime we don't know what to do
even when we know everything

Even if we know everything
We are just not highly celebrated but
Sometimes we don't need super powers
To be celebrated, all it takes is to be yourself
Be like Beethoven and make a symphony about love
Or better yet talk to Venus about love under the moonlight

So as humans,
We spend hours and hours
Socially connected but we are
Emotionally broken and sometimes
As we write, we get blocked from
creativity, but it's all about
What we stand for that makes us
Strong, even though we all crave to have
Power, Gold, Platinum, Silver and Diamonds
We can't have it all
Sometimes all we have is languages
Even when we don't speak the same language
Love should spread
Music and poetry is the best way to
Spread the love but we end up doing it
For the money and we forget the skill it takes
Sometimes all it takes is acceptance

If I could, I would
Give you the moons and stars
Give you the universe
I am of royal blood
even though I sometimes have a
Mafia persona
I will never hurt you
I don't want to see you in pain

So, you asked me
What's death?
And I said
If there's no life without death
then there's no death without life
So, you asked again
What's death
And I said
Death is life
Eternal life
life without end

In the beginning, during the creation phase of this book, I had a different outlook on the book, I even had a different title for the book – [Poetry is Au]. Poetry is Au was the first and initial title for the book but as time went on, I saw the title was not conveying my thoughts and message as clear as I wanted, therefore I began looking for the perfect title that would perfectly fit the content of this book.

"Putting words On paper to Express in part Thoughts from me Right to Your heart"
POETRY

So, as I was looking for the perfect title, I felt like I didn't know what poetry stands for or rather, what poetry means so I broke the word down until I could make sense of what it means. This therefore showed me something rare, that although poets have their own unique ways of expressing themselves at the end of the day, they connected to someone, they saved someone, they were able to be a pillar of support and strength to someone, they were able to educate someone about something [knowledge is power]. What I'm trying to say is that even though "it's just words on paper" those words carry a lot of weight; those words are meaningful even if it's only 6 words [food for the heart and soul].

To me, whoever is a poet should be highly recognized because the main purpose of a poet is to express true thoughts, therefore if the thoughts are true then something unique and special has been created.

One thing about the men who have the pen of history, is that they always seem to write out their sins, but it's time to change that. I'm writing my whole story and I'm not leaving out any detail, if needs be this will help right my wrongs, instead of just writing everything I did right. Everything that I write I'm just keeping it real; some say I am 'too real to be fake', I'm just glad that's how they see me because the world needs more people like that.

Everything has changed, everything seems to be commercialized and I guess it's time for you to take a minute and ask yourself if you are making an impact , a little fact, is that somewhere deep down you have to keep it real, I mean we are all in a quest for something to satisfy our consciousness .Writing this book exposed me to so many things, things which I didn't really know. I guess it makes one aware of their surroundings, I guess books do give knowledge and you know what they say about knowledge – 'knowledge is power'. Keep reading and I hope you enjoyed this book,

Terminologies used

1. **Therapeutic**: therapy to relieve pain (noun)(adjective).

2. **Poemteritis**: poem-ter-it-is [poh-em-te-rite-is] a condition of writing poems non-stop (noun). Example I have poemteristis.

3. **Poetrytis**: poet-ry-tis [poh-at-re-i-tis] a condition of writing poems non-stop (noun). Example I suffer from extreme poetrytis.

4. **Arsenic**: a very poisonous metallic element that has three allotropic forms, an arsenic is a poisonous element that no person or animal should eat and drink. It's a white powdered poison used in manufacturing glass and pesticides.

5. **Asphyxiate**: the condition of being deprived of oxygen (air)

6. **Invocation:** A prayer asking God's help [the act of appealing for help]

7. **Vexed:** Be a mystery of bewildering to

FOOD FOR THE SOUL AND HEART

www.ingramcontent.com/pod-product-compliance
Lightning Source LLC
Chambersburg PA
CBHW021235090426
42740CB00006B/542